NORSE MYTHOLOGY

ODIN

BY KATE CONLEY

Kids Core

An Imprint of Abdo Publishing
abdobooks.com

abdobooks.com

Published by Abdo Publishing, a division of ABDO, PO Box 398166, Minneapolis, Minnesota 55439. Copyright © 2024 by Abdo Consulting Group, Inc. International copyrights reserved in all countries. No part of this book may be reproduced in any form without written permission from the publisher. Kids Core™ is a trademark and logo of Abdo Publishing.

Printed in the United States of America, North Mankato, Minnesota.
052023
092023

THIS BOOK CONTAINS RECYCLED MATERIALS

Cover Photos: Shutterstock Images (background, Odin)
Interior Photos: Culture Club/Bridgeman/Hulton Archive/Getty Images, 4–5; Historic Images/Alamy, 7; North Wind Picture Archives/Alamy, 9; Chronicle/Alamy, 10; Ivy Close Images/Alamy, 12–13, 19, 20, 29 (top), 29 (bottom); Michael Nicholson/Corbis Historical/Getty Images, 14, 28 (top); Science History Images/Alamy, 17, 28 (bottom); Charles Walker Collection/Alamy, 18; Jay Maidment/Marvel Studios/Photo 12/Alamy, 22–23; Janzig/Europe/Alamy, 25; Ulf Bruxe/Swedish History Museum, https://mis.historiska.se/mis/sok/fid.asp?fid=110733, 26

Editor: Katharine Hale
Series Designer: Katharine Hale

Library of Congress Control Number: 2022949117

Publisher's Cataloging-in-Publication Data

Names: Conley, Kate, author.
Title: Odin / by Kate Conley
Description: Minneapolis, Minnesota: Abdo Publishing Company, 2024 | Series: Norse mythology | Includes online resources and index.
Identifiers: ISBN 9781098291211 (lib. bdg.) | ISBN 9781098277390 (ebook)
Subjects: LCSH: Mythology, Norse--Juvenile literature. | Odin (Norse deity)--Juvenile literature. | Gods--Juvenile literature. | Divinities--Juvenile literature.
Classification: DDC 293.13--dc23

CONTENTS

Ymir, Buri, and Audumla are three characters in the Norse creation myth.

CHAPTER 1

THE HIGHEST GOD

In the beginning of time, two worlds existed. Niflheim was in the north. Icy winds blew over this cold, dark world. Muspelheim was in the south. This world glowed with heat and fire. A gap existed between the worlds. This gap is where life began.

The first creature was a giant. His name was Ymir. He survived by drinking the milk of a cow called Audumla. The cow licked salt from stones that were covered in ice. One day, the cow licked a stone that became a man. The man's name was Buri. He became the grandfather of the gods Odin, Vili, and Ve.

Odin, Vili, and Ve killed Ymir. They moved his body to the gap. The brothers used Ymir's body to build new lands. The bones became mountains. The teeth became rocks and sand. The blood became the oceans, and the flesh became soil. The brothers called this new land Midgard.

On a beach in Midgard, the brothers found two logs. Odin breathed life into them. Vili gave

In another version of the Norse creation story, the brothers who create the first humans are Odin, Hoenir, and Lodurr.

the logs the ability to think and move. Ve crafted them into human bodies. He gave them speech, sight, and hearing. The logs were now living human beings. One was a man, and the other was a woman. All humans descended from these two people.

Norse Mythology

This creation myth is thousands of years old. It was a story from the religion of early northern Germanic peoples. Today, the stories from this religion are known as Norse mythology. Most surviving Norse myths were written in the Old Norse language. They come from **Scandinavia**.

Embla and Ask

Odin, Vili, and Ve named the first humans. They called the woman Embla. This means "elm." She was carved from an elm log. They called the man Ask. This means "ash." He was carved from an ash log. Embla, Ask, and their descendants all made their homes in Midgard.

The Norse people told their stories out loud. The stories changed over time.

Norse mythology tells the stories of gods and goddesses, giants, elves, dwarfs, and more. These creatures live across nine worlds. The worlds are connected by a giant tree called Yggdrasil (IHG-druh-sihl).

Yggdrasil and the Nine Worlds

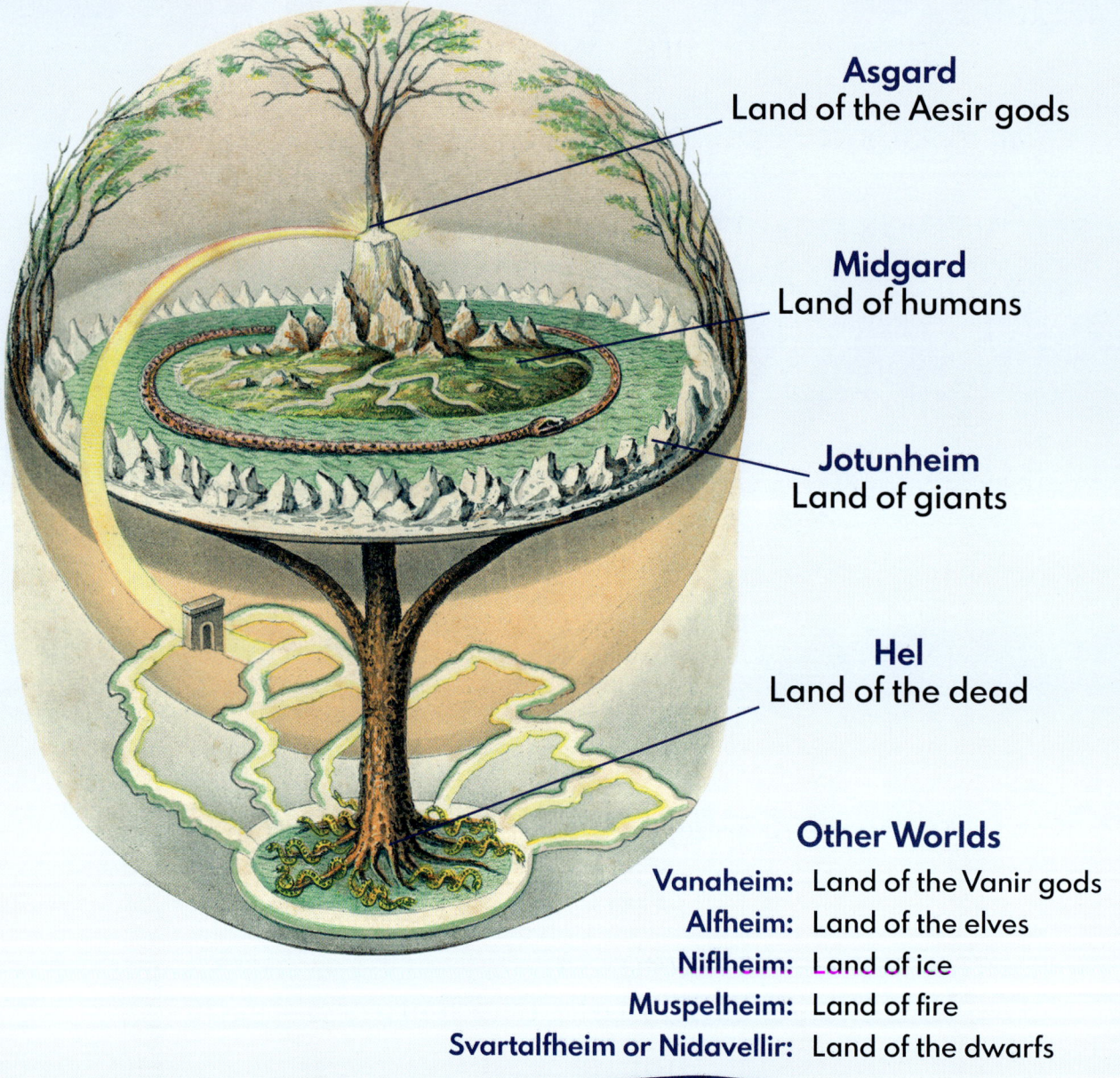

Asgard
Land of the Aesir gods

Midgard
Land of humans

Jotunheim
Land of giants

Hel
Land of the dead

Other Worlds

Vanaheim: Land of the Vanir gods
Alfheim: Land of the elves
Niflheim: Land of ice
Muspelheim: Land of fire
Svartalfheim or Nidavellir: Land of the dwarfs

Because the Norse people were familiar with the nine worlds, Old Norse sources do not give many details about them. This means historians are not exactly sure which worlds are included in the nine or where they are.

Odin was the first god. He was also the highest, most powerful god who ruled all others. This makes him one of the most important figures in Norse mythology. Most descriptions of Odin come from two writings. They are *The Prose Edda* and *The Poetic Edda*. These texts are from the 1200s. They have kept alive the stories about Odin and the other gods.

Further Evidence

Look at the website below. Does it give any new details about the creation story from Chapter One?

Odin Creates the World

abdocorelibrary.com/odin

Odin was the leader of the Norse gods.

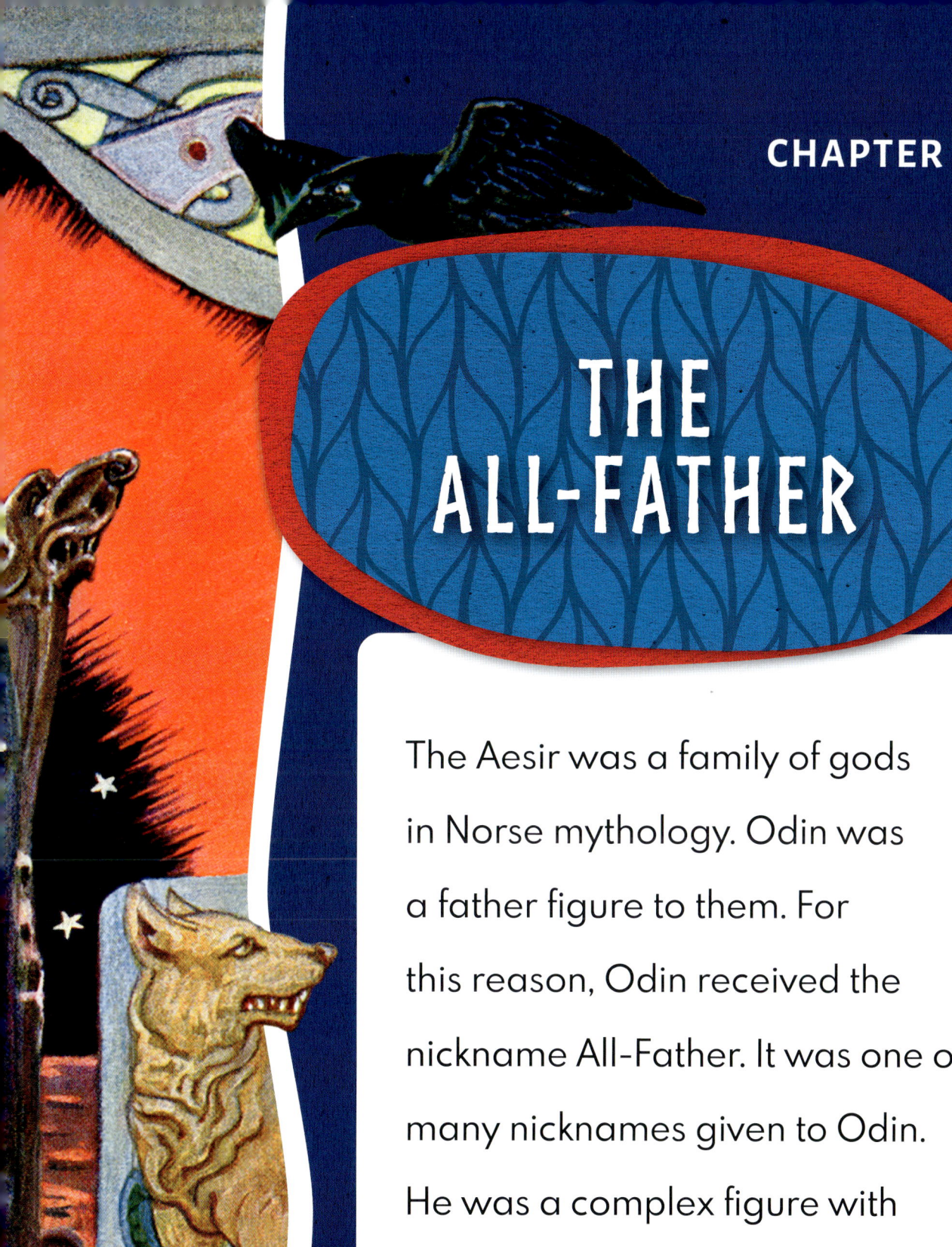

CHAPTER 2

THE ALL-FATHER

The Aesir was a family of gods in Norse mythology. Odin was a father figure to them. For this reason, Odin received the nickname All-Father. It was one of many nicknames given to Odin. He was a complex figure with many roles in Norse mythology.

Frigg is a goddess of marriage who can see the future.

Odin was married to the goddess Frigg. She was a powerful goddess who could see the future. Odin fathered many children with different mothers. His most famous sons were

Thor and Baldr. Thor was the god of thunder and the strongest of all the gods. Baldr was famous for his death at the hands of the **trickster** god Loki.

The gods all lived in Asgard. Odin sat upon a throne in a watchtower called Hlidskjalf. From this spot, Odin kept watch over the world. He could see the deeds of all humans and creatures. A pair of ravens joined Odin on his throne. One raven was named Huginn. This means "thought." The other raven was named Muninn. This means "memory" or "wisdom." Each morning, Odin sent the ravens into the world. They gathered information for him. When the birds returned, they whispered to Odin what they had learned.

Odin also had two wolves. The wolves were tame. Their names were Geri and Freki. Odin fed them from his own plate at mealtimes.

Knowledge and Poetry

Odin was a god of war. He provided magic, protection, and advice to warriors. Odin was a brave warrior himself. He carried a spear

Valkyries

Young women called Valkyries worked for Odin. He sent them to battlefields. Valkyries chose which warriors had died bravely. They took the chosen to Valhalla. It was the hall for **slain** warriors. There, Odin trained them for Ragnarok. The Norse people believed this would be a big battle at the end of the world.

Loki turned into a horse and gave birth to Sleipnir, Odin's eight-legged horse.

called Gungnir. It had been made by dwarfs, who were master crafters. The spear never missed its target. Odin rode a flying horse with eight legs. His name was Sleipnir. Sleipnir was large and fast. He could quickly carry Odin to any of the worlds.

But Odin was more than a warrior. He was also the god of wisdom and knowledge. Mimir's Well was the source of all wisdom. Odin gave up one of his eyes to take a drink from it.

Odin was known for wisdom and poetry as well as battle.

A poem called *Havamal* describes how Odin learned to read runes.

Odin also wanted to learn how to read **runes**. He hung himself from Yggdrasil for nine nights. When he was done, he could read runes. They gave him many powerful spells.

The giantess Gunnlod guarded the mead of poetry. She gave it to Odin to drink.

Odin was also the god of poetry. He became a poet by drinking three jugs of **mead**. The mead was kept by a giant. Odin tricked the giant's daughter into letting him have it. Her father was furious. Odin did not want the giant to catch him. He transformed into an eagle. The giant transformed into an eagle too. He chased Odin. But Odin was faster. Odin returned to Asgard with the skill of poetry. He shared it with the gods and humankind.

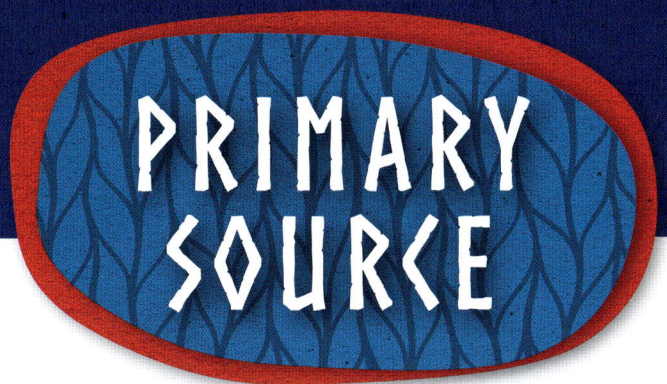

Havamal, or "Words of the One-Eyed," is a poetic collection of Odin's wisdom. Odin says:

> At every doorway
>
> before you enter,
>
> you should look around . . .
>
> for you never know
>
> where your enemies
>
> might be seated within.

Source: Jackson Crawford, translator. *The Poetic Edda: Stories of the Norse Gods and Heroes.* Hackett, 2015, p. 17.

What's the Big Idea?

What is this quote's main idea? Explain how the main idea is supported by details.

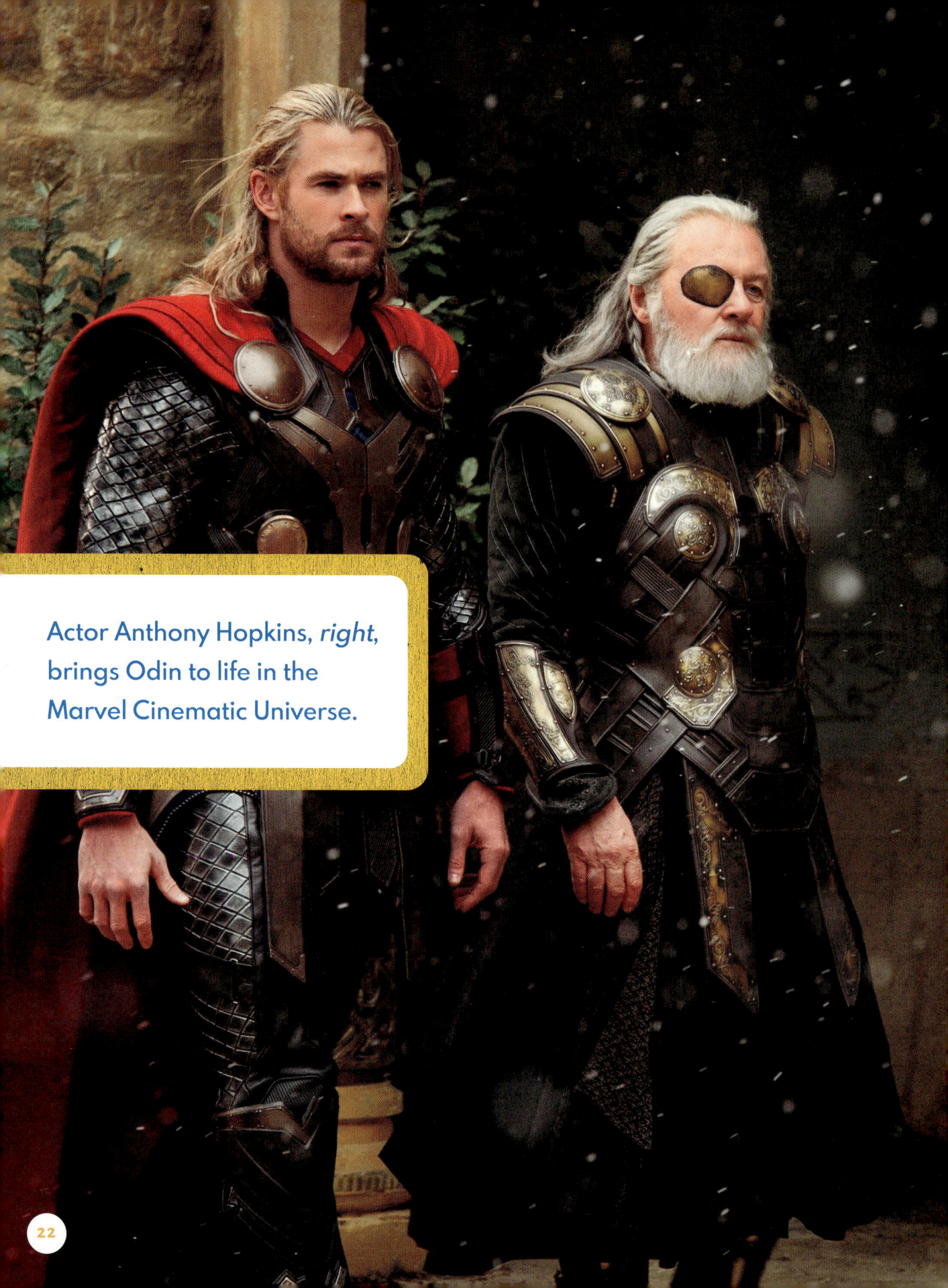

Actor Anthony Hopkins, *right*, brings Odin to life in the Marvel Cinematic Universe.

CHAPTER 3

ODIN'S IMPORTANCE

Norse people worshipped Odin. He had power over many things, from battle to poetry. Norse people viewed him as the creator of human life. He had the power to decide the outcome of wars. He was wise and all knowing. Odin could cast powerful spells.

And he ruled over fallen warriors in his great hall called Valhalla.

Odin had a lot of power. Many Norse people wanted him to favor them. Warriors, kings, and other leaders worshipped him. They made **sacrifices** to Odin. The sacrifices were like a trade. A king might ask Odin for victory in a battle. That king might sacrifice an animal or person to Odin in exchange for the victory.

Wednesday

The Norse people named the days of the week after their gods. One of the many versions of Odin's name is Woden. The day devoted to him was called "Woden's Day." This eventually became *Wednesday*.

Historians believe this stone from Gotland, Sweden, shows the gods Odin, *top right and bottom left,* Thor, and Frey.

Despite his power, Odin was not unstoppable. In Norse mythology, Ragnarok is the end of the world. Stories say there will be a great battle between giants and gods. In the battle, Odin will lead the gods. His soldiers will be the fallen heroes from Valhalla.

Bracteates are thin gold pendants from early Scandinavia. Scholars think bracteates that show a rider with birds could represent Odin.

Odin will face a giant wolf named Fenrir. The wolf will swallow Odin, killing him. Most of the other gods will not survive. When the battle is over, the world will be reborn.

Odin in Art and Today

Odin's power made him a common figure in Norse art. **Figurines**, jewelry, and carvings from Scandinavia show how Norse people saw Odin. Norse artists often showed Odin with his ravens.

He was sometimes holding a spear or riding a horse. Later artists often showed Odin as an old man. In these works, Odin wears a hat and a cape. Odin is pictured with one eye, a flowing beard, and his spear.

Today, Odin is still a well-known figure. He appears in many books, comics, and graphic novels. Odin's stories are very old. But he remains a complex figure of wisdom and power.

Explore Online

Visit the website below. Does it give any new information about the people who worshipped Odin?

Who Were the Vikings?

abdocorelibrary.com/odin

LEGENDARY FACTS

Odin is the ruler of the gods. He is married to Frigg.

Odin rides an eight-legged horse called Sleipnir.

Odin has two ravens, Huginn and Muninn. They bring him news of the world each day. He also has two wolves, Geri and Freki.

Odin took the mead of poetry from the giants.

Glossary

figurines
small statues

mead
an alcoholic drink made of honey and water

runes
alphabetic symbols used by the Norse people and believed to have special powers

sacrifices
offerings to a god

Scandinavia
the countries of Norway, Sweden, and Denmark, and sometimes Iceland and Finland

slain
killed in a violent way

trickster
a person who plays pranks or tricks on someone else

Online Resources

To learn more about Odin, visit our free resource websites below.

Visit **abdocorelibrary.com** or scan this QR code for free Common Core resources for teachers and students, including vetted activities, multimedia, and booklinks, for deeper subject comprehension.

Visit **abdobooklinks.com** or scan this QR code for free additional online weblinks for further learning. These links are routinely monitored and updated to provide the most current information available.

Learn More

Alexander, Heather. *A Child's Introduction to Norse Mythology*. Black Dog & Leventhal, 2018.

Hudak, Heather C. *Valkyries*. Abdo, 2024.

Rea, Amy C. *Frigg*. Abdo, 2024.

Index

About the Author

Kate Conley has been writing nonfiction books for children for more than ten years. When she's not writing, Conley spends her time reading, sewing, and solving crossword puzzles. She lives in Minnesota with her husband and two children.